Stiles

D0168678

UBU REPERTORY THEATER PUBLICATIONS

<u>Individual plays:</u>

* *Swimming Pools at War* by Yves Navarre, 1982.
* *Night Just Before the Forest* and *Struggle of the Dogs and the Black,* by Bernard-Marie Koltès, 1982.
The Fetishist by Michel Tournier, 1983. (Out of print).
* *The Office* by Jean-Paul Aron, 1983.
* *Far From Hagondange* and *Vater Land, the Country of our Fathers* by Jean-Paul Wenzel, 1984.
Deck Chairs by Madeleine Laïk, 1984. (Out of print).
The Passport and *The Door* by Pierre Bourgeade, 1984. (Out of print).
The Showman by Andrée Chedid, 1984. (Out of print).
* *Madame Knipper's Journey to Eastern Prussia* by Jean-Luc Lagarce, 1984.
Family Portrait by Denise Bonal, 1985; new edition, 1992.
Passengers by Daniel Besnehard, 1985. (Out of print).
* *Cabale* by Enzo Cormann, 1985.
Enough is Enough by Protais Asseng, 1986.
Monsieur Thôgô-gnini by Bernard Dadié, 1985.
The Glorious Destiny of Marshal Nnikon Nniku by Tchicaya U Tam'si, 1986.
Parentheses of Blood by Sony Labou Tansi, 1986.
Intelligence Powder by Kateb Yacine, 1986.
The Sea Between Us by Denise Chalem, 1986.
Country Landscapes by Jacques-Pierre Amette, 1986.
Nowhere and *A Man with Women* by Reine Bartève, 1987.
The White Bear by Daniel Besnehard, 1992.
The Best of Schools by Jean-Marie Besset, 1992.
Jock by Jean-Louis Bourdon, 1992.
A Tempest by Aimé Césaire, 1993 (new edition).

Ubu Repertory Theater: 1982-1992, A bilingual illustrated history with personal statements by various playwrights and theater personalities, 1992.

* *Distributed by Ubu Repertory Theater, 15 West 28th Street, New York, NY 10001. All other titles distributed by Theatre Communications Group, 355 Lexington Avenue, New York, NY 10017.*

Anthologies

Afrique I: New plays from the Congo, Ivory Coast, Senegal and Zaire, including *The Daughter of the Gods* by Abdou Anta Kâ, *Equatorium* by Maxime N'Debeka, *Lost Voices* by Diur N'Tumb, *The Second Ark* by Sony Labou Tansi, and *The Eye* by Bernard Zadi Zaourou. Preface by George C. Wolfe. 1987. (Out of print).

The Paris Stage: Recent Plays: *A Birthday Present for Stalin* by Jean Bouchaud, *The Rest Have Got It Wrong* by Jean-Michel Ribes, *The Sleepless City* by Jean Tardieu, *Trumpets of Death* by Tilly, and *The Neighbors* by Michel Vinaver. Preface by Catherine Temerson and Françoise Kourilsky. 1988.

Plays by Women: An International Anthology: *A Picture Perfect Sky* by Denise Bonal, *Jocasta* by Michèle Fabien, *The Girls from the Five and Ten* by Abla Farhoud, *You Have Come Back* by Fatima Gallaire-Bourega, and *Your Handsome Captain* by Simone Schwarz-Bart. Preface by Catherine Temerson and Françoise Kourilsky. 1988, 1991.

Gay Plays: An International Anthology: *The Function* by Jean-Marie Besset, *A Tower Near Paris* and *Grand Finale* by Copi, *Return of the Young Hippolytus* by Hervé Dupuis, *Ancient Boys* by Jean-Claude van Itallie, and *The Lives and Deaths of Miss Shakespeare* by Liliane Wouters. Preface by Catherine Temerson and Françoise Kourilsky. 1989, 1991.

Theater and Politics: An International Anthology: *Black Wedding Candles for Blessed Antigone* by Sylvain Bemba, *A Season in the Congo* by Aimé Césaire, *Burn River Burn* by Jean-Pol Fargeau, *Olympe and the Executioner* by Wendy Kesselman and *Mephisto,* adapted from Klaus Mann by Ariane Mnouchkine. Preface by Erika Munk. 1990.

Afrique II: New Plays from Madagascar, Mauritania and Togo including *The Legend of Wagadu as Seen by Sia Yatabere* by Moussa Diagana, *The Crossroads* by Josué Kossi Efoui, *The Herd* by Charlotte-Arrisoa Rafenomanjato, *The Prophet and the President* by Jean-Luc Raharimanana and *The Singing Tortoise* and *Yevi's Adventures in Monsterland* by Sénouvo Agbota Zinsou. Preface by Henry Louis Gates, Jr. 1991.

Aimé Césaire

A
TEMPEST

Based on Shakespeare's *The Tempest*
Adaptation for a Black Theater

Translated from the French
by **Richard Miller**

Ubu Repertory Theater Publications

Printed in the United States of America, 1992.
Library of Congress Catalogue Card Number: 92-063019
ISBN: 0-913745-40-5

Distributed by Theatre Communications Group,
355 Lexington Avenue, New York, N.Y. 10017.

Price: $8.95

A Tempest, in Richard Miller's translation, had its American premiere at Ubu Repertory Theater, 15 West 28th Street, New York, N.Y. 10001, on October 9, 1991.

Director	Robbie McCauley
Set	Jane Sablow
Lights	Zebedee Collins
Costumes	Carol Ann Pelletier
Musical Director	Tiyé Giraud
Movement Director	Marlies Yearby

CAST, IN ALPHABETICAL ORDER

Ariel	Rafael Baez
Trinculo/Captain	Ron Brice
Caliban	Leon Addison Brown
Stephano	Leo V. Finnie, III
Gonzalo	Clebert Ford
Prospero	Arthur French
Goddess	Tiyé Giraud
Ferdinand	Bryan Hicks
Alonso	Lawrence James
Eshu/Master of Ceremonies	Jasper McGruder
Miranda	Sharon McGruder
Sebastian	Patrick Rameau
Antonio	Kim Sullivan
Goddess	Marlies Yearby

Produced by Ubu Repertory Theater
Françoise Kourilsky, *Artistic Director.*

"The Ubu Repertory Company's production of (Césaire's) play, in a translation by Richard Miller is a sprightly and song-filled enchantment with a first-rate cast under the direction of Robbie McCauley. The luminous intelligence of Mr. Césaire's meditation on the absurdities of colonialism shines through the antics of the bewildered characters."

—The New York Times, October 16, 1991

"Perhaps the most significant accomplishment of A Tempest, where Césaire's script, McCauley's direction, and Giraud's music all come together, is the making of Caliban into a hero through the illumination of his culture."

—The Village Voice, October 22, 1991

"None of Césaire's wry humor or political edge was lost in the Ubu Repertory Company's rendition.... The text was uniformly well-acted.... The calypso songs seemed natural and spontaneous in the Caribbean setting. The costumes and sparse trees-and-rocks scenery were understated, allowing the audience to concentrate on the dialogue. Consequently, despite its overt political purpose, Césaire's *A Tempest* seemed the most true in spirit to Shakespeare's original play."

—Shakespeare Bulletin, Vol. 10, No. 1, Winter 1992

TRANSLATOR'S NOTE

The translation of Aimé Césaire's *Une Tempête* presented more challenges than usually arise in the transfer of a play from one language into another (differences in cultural background, tone, milieu and so on). Although Césaire has denied attempting any linguistic echo of Shakespeare, the transposition of his play into English inevitably calls up such echoes, for the literate English/American playgoer cannot help but "hear," behind the language of the play, the original text resounding in all its well-known beauty, its familiarity. For the translator, therefore, the temptation to quote the Ariel songs, for example, or to paraphrase them, was strong. When Césaire has his Ariel sing of something "proche et étrange," for example, Shakespeare's "rich and strange" must, inevitably, sound in the translator's mind.

I have attempted to avoid temptation (there is, if I recall, only one instance of direct quotation in the prose text, but it fell so aptly into place that I was unable to resist); in the main I have left the (slightly altered) song for Ariel with its Shakespearean references unchanged. In an appendix I have now added a "literal" translation of Césaire's text to give a better notion of the imagery he uses for the character. As for the other songs in the text, the options indicated are extremely free adaptations or indications of what I felt to be the substance of the originals or (as in the case of "Oh, Susannah" and "Blow the Man Down") songs familiar to an English-speaking audience that I thought reflected something of the spirit and possible familiarity of the originals.

For this revised edition, I have also included, as an appendix, a "literal" translation of these songs as they occur in French.

Then there is the question of over-all tone of voice, taken for granted in *The Tempest*, where social classes, the real and the spirit worlds, are a given. In *A Tempest*, with its Caribbean (and therefore colonial) setting and its consecration to a black theater, it is essential, I feel, for the director and the actors to decide what accents, what "classes," they wish the various characters to reflect. In my own head, I have heard Ariel's song, for example, as vaguely calypso; others will have other ideas. The director may also wish to emphasize the "political" aspects of the play, in which case the accents employed by the actors would tend to serve that purpose. In any event, in translating the play I have not tried to indicate accent (other than in the Ariel song) and where slang or obscenities have been employed, the emphasis to be given will be set by the director or actor in the way that will best reflect and enhance the tone and style of the particular production.

CHARACTERS

As in Shakespeare

Two alterations: Ariel, a mulatto slave
                          Caliban, a black slave

An addition: Eshu, a black devil-god

Ambiance of a psychodrama. The actors enter singly, at random, and each chooses for himself a mask at his leisure.

MASTER OF CEREMONIES: Come gentlemen, help yourselves. To each his character, to each character his mask. You, Prospero? Why not? He has reserves of will power he's not even aware of himself. You want Caliban? Well, that's revealing. Ariel? Fine with me. And what about Stephano, Trinculo? No takers? Ah, just in time! It takes all kinds to make a world.

And after all, they aren't the worst characters. No problem about the juvenile leads, Miranda and Ferdinand. You, okay. And there's no problem about the villains either: you, Antonio; you, Alonso, perfect! Oh, Christ! I was forgetting the Gods. Eshu will fit you like a glove. As for the other parts, just take what you want and work it out among yourselves. But make up your minds... Now, there's one part I have to pick out myself: you! It's for the part of the Tempest, and I need a storm to end all storms... I need a really big guy to do the wind. Will you do that? Fine! And then someone strong for Captain of the ship. Good, now let's go. Ready? Begin. Blow, winds! Rain and lightning *ad lib!*

ACT I

SCENE 1

GONZALO: Of course, we're only straws tossed on the raging sea...but all's not lost, Gentlemen. We just have to try to get to the eye of the storm.

ANTONIO: We might have known this old fool would nag us to death!

SEBASTIAN: To the bitter end!

GONZALO: Try to understand what I'm telling you: imagine a huge cylinder like the chimney of a lamp, fast as a galloping horse, but in the center as still and unmoving as Cyclop's eye. That's what we're talking about when we say "the eye of the storm" and that's where we have to get.

ANTONIO: Oh, great! Do you really mean that the cyclone or Cyclops, if he can't see the beam in his own eye, will let us escape! Oh, that's very illuminating!

GONZALO: It's a clever way of putting it, at any rate. Literally false, but yet quite true. But what's the fuss going on up there? The Captain seems worried. *(Calling.)* Captain!

CAPTAIN: *(with a shrug)* Boatswain!

BOATSWAIN: Aye, sir!

CAPTAIN: We're coming round windward of the island. At

this speed we'll run aground. We've got to turn her around. Heave to! *(Exits.)*

BOATSWAIN: Come on, men! Heave to! To the topsail; man the ropes. Pull! Heave ho, heave ho!

ALONSO: *(approaching)* Well, Boatswain, how are things going? Where are we?

BOATSWAIN: If you ask me, you'd all be better off below, in your cabins.

ANTONIO: *He* doesn't seem too happy. We'd better ask the Captain. Where's the Captain, Boatswain? He was here just a moment ago, and now he's gone off.

BOATSWAIN: Get back below where you belong! We've got work to do!

GONZALO: My dear fellow, I can quite understand your being nervous, but a man should be able to control himself in any situation, even the most upsetting.

BOATSWAIN: Shove it! If you want to save your skins, you'd better get yourselves back down below to those first-class cabins of yours.

GONZALO: Now, now, my good fellow, you don't seem to know to whom you're speaking. *(Making introductions.)* The King's brother, the King's son and myself, the King's counsellor.

BOATSWAIN: King! King! Well, there's someone who doesn't give a fuck more about the kind that he does about you or me, and he's called the Gale. His Majesty the Gale! And right now, he's in control and we're all his subjects.

GONZALO: He might just as well be pilot on the ferry to hell...his mouth's foul enough!

ANTONIO: In a sense, the fellow *re*gales me, as you might say. We'll pull through, you'll see, because he looks to me more like someone who'll end up on the gallows, not beneath the billows.

SEBASTIAN: The end result is the same. The fish will get us and the crows will get him.

GONZALO: He did irritate me, rather. However, I take the attenuating circumstances into account...and, you must admit, he lacks neither courage nor wit.

BOATSWAIN: *(returning)* Pull in the stud sails. Helmsman, into the wind! Into the wind!

Enter Sebastian, Antonio, Gonzalo.

BOATSWAIN: You again! If you keep bothering us and don't get below and say your prayers I'll give up and let you sail the ship! You can't expect me to be the go-between for your souls and Beelzebub!

ANTONIO: It's really too much! The fellow is taking advantage of the situation...

4

BOATSWAIN: Windward! Windward! Heave into the wind!

Thunder, lightning.

SEBASTIAN: Ho! Ho!

GONZALO: Did you see that? There, at the top of the masts, in the rigging, that glitter of blue fire, flashing, flashing? They're right when they call these magic lands, so different from our homes in Europe... Look, even the lightning is different!

ANTONIO: Maybe its a foretaste of the hell that awaits us.

GONZALO: You're too pessimistic. Anyway, I've always kept myself in a state of grace, ready to meet my maker.

Sailors enter.

SAILORS: Shit! We're sinking!

The passengers can be heard singing "Nearer, my God, to Thee..."

BOATSWAIN: To leeward! To leeward!

FERDINAND: *(entering)* Alas! There's no one in hell...all the devils are here!

The ship sinks.

SCENE 2

MIRANDA: Oh God! Oh God! A sinking ship! Father, help!

PROSPERO: *(enters hurriedly carrying a megaphone.)* Come daughter, calm yourself! It's only a play. There's really nothing wrong. Anyway, everything that happens is for our own good. Trust me, I won't say any more.

MIRANDA: But such a fine ship, and so many fine, brave lives sunk, drowned, laid waste to wrack and ruin... A person would have to have a heart of stone not to be moved...

PROSPERO: Drowned...hmmm. That remains to be seen. But draw near, dear Princess. The time has come.

MIRANDA: You're making fun of me, father. Wild as I am, you know I am happy — like a queen of the wildflowers, of the streams and paths, running barefoot through thorns and flowers, spared by one, caressed by the other.

PROSPERO: But you are a Princess...for how else does one address the daughter of a Prince? I cannot leave you in ignorance any longer. Milan is the city of your birth, and the city where for many years I was the Duke.

MIRANDA: Then how did we come here? And tell me, too, by what ill fortune did a prince turn into the reclusive hermit you are now, here, on this desert isle? Was it because you found the world distasteful, or through the perfidy of some enemy? Is our island a prison or a hermitage? You've hinted at some mystery so many times and aroused my curiosity, and today you shall tell me all.

PROSPERO: In a way, it is because of all the things you mention. First, it is because of political disagreements, because of the intrigues of my ambitious younger brother. Antonio is his name, your uncle, and Alonso the name of the envious King of Naples. How their ambitions were joined, how my brother became the accomplice of my rival, how the latter promised the former his protection and my throne...the devil alone knows how all that came about. In any event, when they learned that through my studies and experiments I had managed to discover the exact location of these lands for which many had sought for centuries and that I was making preparations to set forth to take possession of them, they hatched a scheme to steal my as-yet-unborn empire from me. They bribed my people, they stole my charts and documents and, to get rid of me, they denounced me to the Inquisition as a magician and sorcerer. To be brief, one day I saw arriving at the palace men to whom I had never granted audience: the priests of the Holy Office.

Flashback: Standing before Prospero, who is wearing his ducal robes, we see a friar reading from a parchment scroll.

THE FRIAR: The Holy Inquisition for the preservation and integrity of the Faith and the pursuit of heretical perversion, acting through the special powers entrusted to it by the Holy Apostolic See, informed of the errors you profess, insinuate and publish against God and his Creation with regard to the shape of the Earth and the possibility of discovering other lands, notwithstanding the fact that the Prophet Isaiah stated and taught that the Lord God is seated upon the circle of the Earth and in its center is Jerusalem and that around the world lies inaccessible Paradise, convinced that it is through wickedness that to support your heresy you quote Strabus, Ptolemy and the tragic author Seneca, thereby lending credence to the notion that profane writings can aspire to an authority equal to that of the most profound of the Holy Scriptures, given your notorious use by both night and day of Arabic calculations and scribblings in Hebrew, Syrian and other demonic tongues and, lastly, given that you have hitherto escaped punishment owing to your temporal authority and have, if not usurped, then transformed that authority and made it into a tyranny, doth hereby strip you of your titles, positions and honors in order that it may then proceed against you according to due process through a full and thorough examination, under which authority we require that you accompany us.

PROSPERO: *(back in the present)* And yet, the trial they said they were going to hold never took place. Such creatures of darkness are too much afraid of the light. To be brief: instead of killing me they chose — even worse — to maroon me here with you on this desert island.

MIRANDA: How terrible, and how wicked the world is! How you must have suffered!

PROSPERO: In all this tale of treason and felony there is but one honorable name: Gonzalo, counsellor to the King of Naples and fit to serve a better master. By furnishing me with food and clothing, by supplying me with my books and instruments, he has done all in his power to make my exile in this disgusting place bearable. And now, through a singular turn, Fortune has brought to these shores the very men involved in the plot against me. My prophetic science had of course already informed me that they would not be content merely with seizing my lands in Europe and that their greed would win out over their cowardice, that they would confront the sea and set out for those lands my genius had discovered. I couldn't let them get away with that, and since I was able to stop them, I did so, with the help of Ariel. We brewed up the storm you have just witnessed, thereby saving my possessions overseas and bringing the scoundrels into my power at the same time.

Enter Ariel.

PROSPERO: Well, Ariel?

ARIEL: Mission accomplished.

PROSPERO: Bravo; good work! But what seems to be the matter? I give you a compliment and you don't seem pleased? Are you tired?

ARIEL: Not tired; disgusted. I obeyed you but — well, why not come out with it? — I did so most unwillingly. It was a real pity to see that great ship go down, so full of life.

PROSPERO: Oh, so you're upset, are you! It's always like that with you intellectuals! Who cares! What interests me is not your moods, but your deeds. Let's split: I'll take the zeal and you can keep your doubts. Agreed?

ARIEL: Master, I must beg you to spare me this kind of labour.

PROSPERO: *(shouting)* Listen, and listen good! There's a task to be performed, and I don't care how it gets done!

ARIEL: You've promised me my freedom a thousand times, and I'm still waiting.

PROSPERO: Ingrate! And who freed you from Sycorax, may I ask? Who rent the pine in which you had been imprisoned and brought you forth?

ARIEL: Sometimes I almost regret it... After all, I might have turned into a real tree in the end... Tree: that's a word that really gives me a thrill! It often springs to mind: palm tree — springing into the sky like a fountain ending in nonchalant, squid-like elegance. The baobab — twisted like the soft entrails of some monster. Ask the calao bird that lives a cloistered season in its branches. Or the Ceiba tree — spread out beneath the proud sun. O bird, o green mansions set in the living earth!

PROSPERO: Stuff it! I don't like talking trees. As for your freedom, you'll have it when I'm good and ready. In the meanwhile, see to the ship. I'm going to have a few words with Master Caliban. I've been keeping my eye on him, and he's getting a little too emancipated. *(Calling)* Caliban! Caliban! *(He sighs.)*

Enter Caliban.

CALIBAN: Uhuru!

PROSPERO: What did you say?

CALIBAN: I said, Uhuru!

PROSPERO: Mumbling your native language again! I've already told you, I don't like it. You could be polite, at least; a simple "hello" wouldn't kill you.

CALIBAN: Oh, I forgot... But make that as froggy, waspish, pustular and dung-filled "hello" as possible. May today hasten by a decade the day when all the birds of the sky and beasts of the earth will feast upon your corpse!

PROSPERO: Gracious as always, you ugly ape! How can anyone be so ugly?

CALIBAN: You think I'm ugly...well, I don't think you're so handsome yourself. With that big hooked nose, you look just like some old vulture. *(Laughing)* An old vulture with a scrawny neck!

PROSPERO: Since you're so fond of invective, you could at least thank me for having taught you to speak at all. You, a savage...a dumb animal, a beast I educated, trained, dragged up from the bestiality that still clings to you.

CALIBAN: In the first place, that's not true. You didn't teach me a thing! Except to jabber in your own language so that I could understand your orders: chop the wood, wash the dishes, fish for food, plant vegetables, all because you're too lazy to do it yourself. And as for your learning, did you ever impart any of *that* to me? No, you took care not to. All your science you keep for yourself alone, shut up in those big books.

PROSPERO: What would you be without me?

CALIBAN: Without you? I'd be the king, that's what I'd be, the King of the Island. The king of the island given me by my mother, Sycorax.

PROSPERO: There are some family trees it's better not to climb! She's a ghoul! A witch from whom — and may God be praised — death has delivered us.

CALIBAN: Dead or alive, she was my mother, and I won't deny her! Anyhow, you only think she's dead because you think the earth itself is dead... It's so much simpler that way! Dead, you can walk on it, pollute it, you can tread upon it with the steps of a conqueror. I respect the earth, because I know that it is alive, and I know that Sycorax is alive.
Sycorax. Mother.
Serpent, rain, lightning.
And I see thee everywhere!
In the eye of the stagnant pool which stares back at me,
through the rushes,
in the gesture made by twisted root and its awaiting thrust.
In the night, the all-seeing blinded night,
the nostril-less all-smelling night!
...Often, in my dreams, she speaks to me and warns me...

12

Yesterday, even, when I was lying by the stream on my belly lapping at the muddy water, when the Beast was about to spring upon me with that huge stone in his hand...

PROSPERO: If you keep on like that even your magic won't save you from punishment!

CALIBAN: That's right, that's right! In the beginning, the gentleman was all sweet talk: dear Caliban here, my little Caliban there! And what do you think you'd have done without me in this strange land? Ingrate! I taught you the trees, fruits, birds, the seasons, and now you don't give a damn... Caliban the animal, Caliban the slave! I know that story! Once you've squeezed the juice from the orange, you toss the rind away!

PROSPERO: Oh!

CALIBAN: Do I lie? Isn't it true that you threw me out of your house and made me live in a filthy cave. The ghetto!

PROSPERO: It's easy to say "ghetto"! It wouldn't be such a ghetto if you took the trouble to keep it clean! And there's something you forgot, which is that what forced me to get rid of you was your lust. Good God, you tried to rape my daughter!

CALIBAN: Rape! Rape! Listen, you old goat, you're the one that put those dirty thoughts in my head. Let me tell you something: I couldn't care less about your daughter, or about your cave, for that matter. If I gripe, it's on principle, because I didn't like living with you at all, as a matter of fact.

Your feet stink!

PROSPERO: I did not summon you here to argue. Out! Back to work! Wood, water, and lots of both! I'm expecting company today.

CALIBAN: I've had just about enough. There's already a pile of wood that high...

PROSPERO: Enough! Careful, Caliban! If you keep grumbling you'll be whipped. And if you don't step lively, if you keep dragging your feet or try to strike or sabotage things, I'll beat you. Beating is the only language you really understand. So much the worse for you: I'll speak it, loud and clear. Get a move on!

CALIBAN: All right, I'm going...but this is the last time. It's the last time, do you hear me? Oh...I forgot: I've got something important to tell you.

PROSPERO: Important? Well, out with it.

CALIBAN: It's this: I've decided I don't want to be called Caliban any longer.

PROSPERO: What kind of rot is that? I don't understand.

CALIBAN: Put it this way: I'm *telling* you that from now on I won't answer to the name Caliban.

PROSPERO: Where did you get that idea?

CALIBAN: Well, because Caliban *isn't* my name. It's as simple as that.

PROSPERO: Oh, I suppose it's mine!

CALIBAN: It's the name given me by your hatred, and everytime it's spoken it's an insult.

PROSPERO: My, aren't we getting sensitive! All right, suggest something else... I've got to call you something. What will it be? Cannibal would suit you, but I'm sure you wouldn't like that, would you? Let's see...what about Hannibal? That fits. And why not...they all seem to like historical names.

CALIBAN: Call me X. That would be best. Like a man without a name. Or, to be more precise, a man whose name has been stolen. You talk about history...well, that's history, and everyone knows it! Every time you summon me it reminds me of a basic fact, the fact that you've stolen everything from me, even my identity! Uhuru! *(He exits.)*

Enter Ariel as a sea-nymph.

PROSPERO: My dear Ariel, did you see how he looked at me, that glint in his eye? That's something new. Well, let me tell you, Caliban is the enemy. As for those people on the boat, I've changed my mind about them. Give them a scare, but for God's sake don't touch a hair of their heads! You'll answer to me if you do.

ARIEL: I've suffered too much myself for having made

them suffer not to be pleased at your mercy. You can count on me, Master.

PROSPERO: Yes, however great their crimes, if they repent you can assure them of my forgiveness. They are men of my race, and of high rank. As for me, at my age one must rise above disputes and quarrels and think about the future. I have a daughter. Alonso has a son. If they were to fall in love, I would give my consent. Let Ferdinand marry Miranda, and may their marriage bring us harmony and peace. That is my plan. I want it executed. As for Caliban, does it matter what that villain plots against me? All the nobility of Italy, Naples and Milan henceforth combined, will protect me bodily. Go!

ARIEL: Yes, Master. Your orders will be fully carried out.

Ariel sings:

> *Sandy seashore, deep blue sky,*
> *Surf is rising, sea birds fly*
> *Here the lover finds delight,*
> *Sun at noontime, moon at night.*
> *Join hands lovers, join the dance,*
> *Find contentment, find romance.*
>
> *Sandy seashore, deep blue sky,*
> *Cares will vanish...so can I...*

FERDINAND: What is this music? It has led me here and now it stops... No, there it is again...

ARIEL: *(singing)*

> *Waters move, the ocean flows,*
> *Nothing comes and nothing goes...*
> *Strange days are upon us...*
>
> *Oysters stare through pearly eyes*
> *Heart-shaped corals gently beat*
> *In the crystal undersea*
>
> *Waters move and ocean flows,*
> *Nothing comes and nothing goes...*
> *Strange days are upon us...*

FERDINAND: What is this that I see before me? A goddess? A mortal?

MIRANDA: I know what *I'm* seeing: a flatterer. Young man, your ability to pay compliments in the situation in which you find yourself at least proves your courage. Who are you?

FERDINAND: As you see, a poor shipwrecked soul.

MIRANDA: But one of high degree!

FERDINAND: In other surroundings I might be called "Prince," "son of the King"... But, no, I was forgetting...not "Prince" but "King," alas..."King" because my father has just perished in the shipwreck.

MIRANDA: Poor young man! Here, you'll be received with hospitality and we'll support you in your misfortune.

FERDINAND: Alas, my father... Can it be that I am an unnatural son? Your pity would make the greatest of sorrows seem sweet.

MIRANDA: I hope you'll like it here with us. The island is pretty. I'll show you the beaches and the forests, I'll tell you the names of fruits and flowers, I'll introduce you to a whole world of insects, of lizards of every hue, of birds... Oh, you cannot imagine! The birds!...

PROSPERO: That's enough, daughter! I find your chatter irritating...and let me assure you, it's not at all fitting. You are doing too much honor to an impostor. Young man, you are a traitor, a spy, and a woman-chaser to boot! No sooner has he escaped the perils of the sea than he's sweet-talking the first girl he meets! You won't get round me that way. Your arrival is convenient, because I need more manpower: you shall be my house servant.

FERDINAND: Seeing the young lady, more beautiful than any wood-nymph, I might have been Ulysses on Nausicaa's isle. But hearing you, Sir, I now understand my fate a little better...I see I have come ashore on the Barbary Coast and am in the hands of a cruel pirate. (Drawing his sword) However, a gentleman prefers death to dishonor! I shall defend my life with my freedom!

PROSPERO: Poor fool: your arm is growing weak, your knees are trembling! Traitor! I could kill you now...but I need the manpower. Follow me.

ARIEL: It's no use trying to resist, young man. My master

is a sorcerer: neither your passion nor your youth can prevail against him. Your best course would be to follow and obey him.

FERDINAND: Oh God! What sorcery is this? Vanquished, a captive — yet far from rebelling against my fate, I am finding my servitude sweet. Oh, I would be imprisoned for life if only heaven will grant me a glimpse of my sun each day, the face of my own sun. Farewell, Nausicaa.

They exit.

ACT II

SCENE 1

*Caliban's cave. Caliban is singing as he works when Ariel
enters. He listens to him for a moment.*

CALIBAN: *(singing)*

> *May he who eats his corn heedless of Shango
> Be accursed! May Shango creep beneath
> His nails and eat into his flesh!
> Shango, Shango ho!*
>
> *Forget to give him room if you dare!
> He will make himself at home on your nose!*
>
> *Refuse to have him under your roof at your
> own risk!
> He'll tear off your roof and wear it as a hat!
> Whoever tries to mislead Shango
> Will suffer for it!
> Shango, Shango ho!*

ARIEL: Greetings, Caliban. I know you don't think much of
me, but after all we *are* brothers, brothers in suffering and
slavery, but brothers in hope as well. We both want our
freedom. We just have different methods.

CALIBAN: Greetings to you. But you didn't come to see me
just to make that profession of faith. Come on, Alastor! The
old man sent you, didn't he? A great job: carrying out the

20

Master's fine ideas, his great plans.

ARIEL: No, I've come on my own. I came to warn you. Prospero is planning horrible acts of revenge against you. I thought it my duty to alert you.

CALIBAN: I'm ready for him.

ARIEL: Poor Caliban, you're doomed. You know that you aren't the stronger, you'll never be the stronger. What good will it do you to struggle?

CALIBAN: And what about you? What good has your obedience done you, your Uncle Tom patience and your sucking up to him. The man's just getting more demanding and despotic day by day.

ARIEL: Well, I've at least achieved one thing: he's promised me my freedom. In the distant future, of course, but it's the first time he's actually committed himself.

CALIBAN: Talk's cheap! He'll promise you a thousand times and take it back a thousand times. Anyway, tomorrow doesn't interest me. What I want is *(shouting)* "Freedom now!"

ARIEL: Okay. But you know you're not going to get it out of him "now", and that he's stronger than you are. I'm in a good position to know just what he's got in his arsenal.

CALIBAN: The stronger? How do you know that? Weakness always has a thousand means and cowardice is all that keeps us from listing them.

ARIEL: I don't believe in violence.

CALIBAN: What *do* you believe in, then? In cowardice? In giving up? In kneeling and groveling? That's it, someone strikes you on the right cheek and you offer the left. Someone kicks you on the left buttock and you turn the right...that way there's no jealousy. Well, that's not Caliban's way...

ARIEL: You know very well that that's not what I mean. No violence, no submission either. Listen to me: Prospero is the one we've got to change. Destroy his serenity so that he's finally forced to acknowledge his own injustice and put an end to it.

CALIBAN: Oh sure...that's a good one! Prospero's conscience! Prospero is an old scoundrel who has no conscience.

ARIEL: Exactly — that's why it's up to us to give him one. I'm not fighting just for *my* freedom, for *our* freedom, but for Prospero too, so that Prospero can acquire a conscience. Help me, Caliban.

CALIBAN: Listen, kid, sometimes I wonder if you aren't a little bit nuts. So that Prospero can acquire a conscience? You might as well ask a stone to grow flowers.

ARIEL: I don't know what to do with you. I've often had this inspiring, uplifting dream that one day Prospero, you, me, we would all three set out, like brothers, to build a wonderful world, each one contributing his own special thing: patience, vitality, love, will-power too, and rigor, not to mention the dreams without which mankind would perish.

CALIBAN: You don't understand a thing about Prospero. He's not the collaborating type. He's a guy who only feels something when he's wiped someone out. A crusher, a pulveriser, that's what he is! And you talk about brotherhood!

ARIEL: So then what's left? War? And you know that when it comes to that, Prospero is invincible.

CALIBAN: Better death than humiliation and injustice. Anyhow, I'm going to have the last word. Unless nothingness has it. The day when I begin to feel that everything's lost, just let me get hold of a few barrels of your infernal powder and as you fly around up there in your blue skies you'll see this island, my inheritance, my work, all blown to smithereens...and, I trust, Prospero and me with it. I hope you'll like the fireworks display — it'll be signed Caliban.

ARIEL: Each of us marches to his own drum. You follow yours. I follow the beat of mine. I wish you courage, brother.

CALIBAN: Farewell, Ariel, my brother, and good luck.

SCENE 2

GONZALO: A magnificent country! Bread hangs from the trees and the apricots are bigger than a woman's full breast.

SEBASTIAN: A pity that it's so wild and uncultivated...here and there.

GONZALO: Oh, that's nothing. If there were anything poisonous, an antidote would never be far away, for nature is intrinsically harmonious. I've even read somewhere that guano is excellent compost for sterile ground.

SEBASTIAN: Guano? What kind of animal is that? Are you sure you don't mean iguana?

GONZALO: Young man, if I say guano, I mean guano. Guano is the name for bird-droppings that build up over centuries, and it is by far the best fertilizer known. You dig it out of caves... If you want my opinion, I think we should investigate all the caves on this island one by one to see if we find any, and if we do, this island, if wisely exploited, will be richer than Egypt with its Nile.

ANTONIO: Let me understand: your guano cave contains a river of dried bird-shit.

GONZALO: To pick up your image, all we need to do is channel that river, use it to irrigate, if I may use the term, the fields with this wonderful fecal matter, and everything will bloom.

SEBASTIAN: But we'll still need manpower to farm it. Is the island even inhabited?

GONZALO: That's the problem, of course. But if it is, it must be by wonderful people. It's obvious: a wondrous land can only contain wonderful creatures.

ANTONIO: Yes!

> *Men whose bodies are wiry and strong*
> *And women whose eyes are open and frank...*
> *creatures in it!...*

GONZALO: Something like that! I see you know your literature. But in that case, watch out: it will all mean new responsibilities for us!

SEBASTIAN: How do you get that?

GONZALO: I mean that if the island is inhabited, as I believe, and if we colonize it, as is my hope, then we have to take every precaution not to import our shortcomings, yes, what we call civilization. They must stay as they are: savages, noble and good savages, free, without any complexes or complications. Something like a pool granting eternal youth where we periodically come to restore our aging, citified souls.

ALONSO: Sir Gonzalo, when will you shut up?

GONZALO: Ah, Your Majesty, if I am boring you, I apologize. I was only speaking as I did to distract you and to turn our sad thoughts to something more pleasant. There, I'll be silent. Indeed, these old bones have had it. Oof! Let me sit down...with your permission, of course.

ALONSO: Noble Old Man, even though younger than you, we are all in the same fix.

GONZALO: In other words, dead tired and dying of hunger.

ALONSO: I have never pretended to be above the human condition.

A strange, solemn music is heard.

...Listen, listen! Did you hear that?

GONZALO: Yes, it's an odd melody!

> *Prospero enters, invisible. Other strange figures enter as well, bearing a laden table. They dance and graciously invite the King and his company to eat, then they disappear.*

ALONSO: Heaven protect us! Live marionettes!

GONZALO: Such grace! Such music! Hum. The whole thing is most peculiar.

SEBASTIAN: Gone! Faded away! But what does that matter, since they've left their food behind! No meal was ever more welcome. Gentlemen, to table!

ALONSO: Yes, let us partake of this feast, even though it may be our last.

They prepare to eat, but Elves enter and, with much grimacing and many contortions, carry off the table.

GONZALO: Ah! that's a fine way to behave!

ALONSO: I have the distinct feeling that we have fallen under the sway of powers that are playing at cat and mouse with us. It's a cruel way to make us aware of our dependent status.

GONZALO: The way things have been going it's not surprising, and it will do us no good to protest.

The Elves return, bringing the food with them.

ALONSO: Oh no, this time I won't bite!

SEBASTIAN: I'm so hungry that I don't care, I'll abandon my scruples..

GONZALO: *(to Alonso)* Why not try? Perhaps the Powers controlling us saw how disappointed we were and took pity on us. After all, even though disappointed a hundred times, Tantalus still tried a hundred times.

ALONSO: ` That was also his torture. I won't touch that food.

PROSPERO: *(invisible)* Ariel, I don't like his refusing.

Harass them until they eat.

ARIEL: Why should we go to any trouble for them? If they won't eat, they can die of hunger.

PROSPERO: No, I *want* them to eat.

ARIEL: That's despotism. A while ago you made me snatch it away just when they were about to gobble it up, and now that they don't want it you are ready to force feed them.

PROSPERO: Enough hairsplitting! My mood has changed! They insult me by not eating. They must be made to eat out of my hand like chicks. That is a sign of submission I insist they give me.

ARIEL: It's evil to play with their hunger as you do with their anxieties and their hopes.

PROSPERO: That is how power is measured. I am Power.

Alonso and his group eat.

ALONSO: Alas, when I think...

GONZALO: That's your trouble, Sire: you think too much.

ALONSO: And thus I should not even think of my lost son! My throne! My country!

GONZALO: *(eating)* Your son! What's to say we won't find him again! As for the rest of it... Look, Sire, this filthy hole is now our entire world. Why seek further? If your thoughts are too vast, cut them down to size.

They eat.

ALONSO: So be it! But I would prefer to sleep. To sleep and to forget.

GONZALO: Good idea! Let's put up our hammocks!

They sleep.

SCENE 3

ANTONIO: Look at those leeches, those slugs! Wallowing in their slime and their snot: Idiots, slime — they're like beached jellyfish.

SEBASTIAN: Shhh! It's the King. And that old graybeard is his venerable counsellor.

ANTONIO: The King is he who watches over his flock when they sleep. That one isn't watching over anything. Ergo, he's not the King. *(Brusquely)* You're really a bloodless lily-liver if you can see a king asleep without getting certain ideas...

SEBASTIAN: I mustn't have any blood, only water.

ANTONIO: Don't insult water. Every time I look at myself I think I'm more handsome, more *there*. My inner juices have always given me my greatness, my true greatness...not the greatness men grant me.

SEBASTIAN: All right, so I'm stagnant water.

ANTONIO: Water is never stagnant. It works, it works in us. It is what gives man his dimension, his true one. Believe me, you're mistaken if you don't grab the opportunity when it's offered you. It may never come again.

SEBASTIAN: What are you getting at? I have a feeling I can guess.

ANTONIO: Guess, guess! Look at that tree swaying in the

wind. It's called a coconut palm. My dear Sebastian, in my opinion it's time to shake the coconut palm.

SEBASTIAN: Now I really don't understand.

ANTONIO: What a dope! Consider my position: I'm Duke of Milan. Well, I wasn't always...I had an older brother. That was Duke Prospero. And if I'm now Duke Antonio, it's because I knew when to shake the coconut palm.

SEBASTIAN: And Prospero?

ANTONIO: What do you mean by that? When you shake a tree, someone is bound to fall. And obviously it wasn't me who fell, because here I am: to assist and serve you, Majesty!

SEBASTIAN: Enough! He's my brother! My scruples won't allow me to... You take care of him while I deal with the old Counsellor.

They draw their swords.

ARIEL: Stop, ruffians! Resistance is futile: your swords are enchanted and falling from your hands!

ANTONIO, SEBASTIAN: Alas! Alas!

ARIEL: Sleepers, awake! Awake, I say! Your life depends on it. With these fine fellows with their long teeth and swords around, anyone who sleeps too soundly risks sleeping forever.

Alonso and Gonzalo awaken.

ALONSO: *(rubbing his eyes)* What's happening? I was asleep, and I was having a terrible dream!

ARIEL: No, you were not dreaming. These fine lords here are criminals who were about to perpetrate the most odious of crimes upon you. Yes, Alonso, you may well marvel that a god should fly to your aid. Were to heaven you deserved it more!

ALONSO: I have never been wanting in respect for the divinity...

ARIEL: I don't know what effect my next piece of news will have on you: The name of him who has sent me to you is Prospero.

ALONSO: Prospero! God save us! *(He falls to his knees.)*

ARIEL: I understand your feelings. He lives. It is he who reigns over this isle, as he reigns over the spirits of the air you breathe... But rise... You need fear no longer. He has not saved your lives to destroy them. Your repentance will suffice, for I can see that it is deep and sincere. *(To Antonio and Sebastian)* As for you, Gentlemen, my master's pardon extends to you as well, on the condition that you renounce your plans, knowing them to be vain.

SEBASTIAN: *(To Antonio)* We could have got worse!

ANTONIO: If it were men we were up against, no one

could make me withdraw, but when it's demons and magic there's no shame in giving in. *(To Ariel)* ...We are the Duke's most humble and obedient servants. Please beg him to accept our thanks.

GONZALO: Oh, how ignoble! How good of you to just wipe the slate clean! No surface repentance...not only do you want attrition, you want contrition as well! Why look at me as though you didn't know what I was talking about? *Attrition:* A selfish regret for offending God, caused by a fear of punishment. *Contrition:* An unselfish regret growing out of sorrow at displeasing God.

ARIEL: Honest Gonzalo, thank you for your clarification. Your eloquence has eased my mission and your pedagogical skill has abbreviated it, for in a few short words you have expressed my master's thought. May your words be heard! Therefore, let us turn the page. To terminate this episode, I need only convoke you all, on my master's behalf, to the celebrations that this very day will mark the engagement of his daughter, Miranda. Alonso, that's good news for you...

ALONSO: What — my son?

ARIEL: Correct. Saved by my master from the fury of the waves.

ALONSO: *(falling to his knees)* God be praised for this blessing more than all the rest. Rank, fortune, throne, I am prepared to forgo all if my son is returned to me...

ARIEL: Come, Gentlemen, follow me.

ACT III

SCENE 1

FERDINAND: *(hoeing and singing)*

> How life has changed
> Now, hoe in hand
> I work away all day...
>
> Hoeing all the day,
> I go my weary way...

CALIBAN: Poor kid! What would he say if he was Caliban! He works night and day, and when he sings, it's

> Oo-en-day, Oo-en-day, Oo-en-day, Macaya...

And no pretty girl to console him! *(Sees Miranda approaching.)* Aha! Let's listen to this!

FERDINAND: *(singing)*

> How life has changed
> Now, hoe in hand ,
> I work away all day...

MIRANDA: Poor young man! Can I help you? You don't look like you were cut out for this kind of work!

FERDINAND: One word from you would be more help to me than anything in the world.

MIRANDA: One word? From me? I must say, I...

FERDINAND: Your name — that's all: What is your name?

MIRANDA: That, I cannot do! It's impossible. My father has expressly forbidden it!

FERDINAND: It is the only thing I long for.

MIRANDA: But I can't, I tell you; it's forbidden!

CALIBAN: *(taking advantage of Miranda's momentary distraction, he whispers her name to Ferdinand.)* Mi-ran-da!

FERDINAND: All right then, I shall christen you with a name of my own. I will call you Miranda.

MIRANDA: That's too much! What a low trick! You must have heard my father calling me... Unless it was that awful Caliban who keeps pursuing me and calling out my name in his stupid dreams!

FERDINAND: No, Miranda... I had only to allow my eyes to speak, as you your face.

MIRANDA: Sssh! My father's coming! He'd better not catch you trying to sweet talk me...

FERDINAND: *(Goes back to work, singing.)*

> *But times have changed*
> *Now, hoeing all the day,*
> *I go my weary way...*

PROSPERO: That's fine, young man! You've managed to accomplish a good deal for a beginning! I see I've misjudged you. But you won't be the loser if you serve me well. Listen, my young friend, there are three things in life: Work, Patience, Continence, and the world is yours... Hey, Caliban, I'm taking this boy away with me. He's done enough for one day. But since the job is urgent, see that it gets finished.

CALIBAN: Me?

PROSPERO: Yes, you! You've cheated me enough with your loafing and fiddling around, so you can work a double shift for once!

CALIBAN: I don't see why I should do someone else's job!

PROSPERO: Who's the boss here? You or me? Listen, monster: if you don't like work, I'll see to it you change your mind!

Prospero and Ferdinand move away.

CALIBAN: Go on, go on...I'll get you one day, you bastard! *(He sets to work, singing.)*

"*Oo-en-day, Oo-en-day, Oo-en-day, Macaya...*"

Shit, now it's raining! As if things weren't bad enough...*(Suddenly, at the sound of a voice, Caliban stiffens.)* Do you hear that, boy? That voice through the storm. Bah! It's Ariel. No, that's not his voice. Whose, then? With an old coot like Prospero... One of his cops, probably. Oh, fine! Now, I'm for it. Men and the elements both against me. Well, the hell with it...I'm used to it. Patience! I'll get them yet. In the meantime better make myself scarce! Let Prospero and his storm and his cops go by ..let the seven maws of Malediction bay!

SCENE 2

Enter Trinculo

TRINCULO: *(singing)*

> *Oh Susannah...oh don't you cry for me... (Etc.)*

You can say that again! My dearest Susannah...trust
Trinculo, we've had all the roaring storms we need, and
more! I swear: the whole crew wiped out, liquidated...
Nothing! Nothing left...! Nothing but poor wandering and
wailing Trinculo! No question about it, it'll be a while
before anyone persuades me to depart from affectionate
women and friendly towns to go off to brave roaring storms!
How it's raining! *(Notices Caliban underneath the wheelbarrow.)*
Ah, an Indian! Dead or alive? You never know with these
tricky races. Yukkk! Anyhow, this will do me fine. If he's
dead, I can use his clothes for shelter, for a coat, a tent, a
covering. If he's alive I'll make him my prisoner and take
him back to Europe and then, by golly, my fortune will be
made! I'll sell him to a carnival. No! I'll show him myself at
fairs! What a stroke of luck! I'll just settle in here where it's
warm and let the storm rage! *(He crawls under cover, back to
back with Caliban.)*

> *Enter Stephano.*

STEPHANO: *(singing)*

> *Blow the man down, hearties,*
> *Blow the man down... (Etc.)*

(Takes a swig of his bottle and continues.)

Blow, blow, blow the man down...(Etc.)

Fortunately, there's still a little wine left in this bottle...enough to give me courage! Be of good cheer, Stephano, where there's life there's thirst...and vice versa! *(Suddenly spies Caliban's head sticking out of the covers.)* My God, on Stephano's word, it looks like a Nindian! *(Comes nearer)* And that's just what it is! A Nindian. That's neat. I really am lucky. There's money to be made from a Nindian like that. If you showed him at a carnival...along with the bearded lady and the flea circus, a real Nindian! An authentic Nindian from the Caribbean! That means real dough, or I'm the last of the idiots! *(Touching Caliban)* But he's ice cold! I don't know what the body temperature of a Nindian is, but this one seems pretty cold to me! Let's hope he's not going to croak! How's that for bad luck: You find a Nindian and he dies on you! A fortune slips through your fingers! But wait, I've got an idea...a good swig of this booze between his lips, that'll warm him up. *(He gives Caliban a drink.)* Look... he's better already. The little glutton even wants some more! Just a second, just a second! *(He walks around the wheelbarrow and sees Trinculo's head sticking out from under the covering.)* Jeez! I must be seeing things! A Nindian with two heads! Shit! If I have to pour drink down *two* gullets I won't have much left for myself! Well, never mind. It's incredible...your everyday Nindian is already something, but one with two heads...a Siamese-twin Nindian, a Nindian with two heads and eight paws, that's really something! My fortune is made. Come on, you wonderful monster, you...let's get a look at your other head! *(He draws nearer to*

Trinculo.) Hello! That face reminds me of something! That nose that shines like a lighthouse...

TRINCULO: That gut...

STEPHANO: That nose looks familiar...

TRINCULO: That gut — there can't be two of them in this lousy world!

STEPHANO: Oh-my-gawd, oh-my-gawd, oh-my-gawd...*that's* it...it's that crook Trinculo!

TRINCULO: Good lord! It's Stephano!

STEPHANO: So, Trinculo, you were saved too... It almost makes you believe God looks after drunks...

TRINCULO: Huh! God...Bacchus, maybe. As a matter of fact, I reached these welcoming shores by floating on a barrel...

STEPHANO: And I by floating on my stomach...it's nearly the same thing. But what kind of creature is this? Isn't it a Nindian?

TRINCULO: That's just what I was thinking... Yes, by God, it's a Nindian. That's a piece of luck...he'll be our guide.

STEPHANO: Judging from the way he can swill it down, he doesn't seem to be stupid. I'll try to civilize him. Oh...not too much, of course. But enough so that he can be of some use.

TRINCULO: Civilize him! Shee-it! Does he even know how to talk?

STEPHANO: I couldn't get a word out of him, but I know a way to loosen his tongue. *(He takes a bottle from his pocket.)*

TRINCULO: *(stopping him)* Look here, you're not going to waste that nectar on the first savage that comes along, are you?

STEPHANO: Selfish! Back off! Let me perform my civilizing mission. *(Offering the bottle to Caliban.)* Of course, if he was cleaned up a bit he'd be worth more to both of us. Okay? We'll exploit him together? It's a deal? *(To Caliban)* Drink up, pal. You. Drink... Yum-yum botty botty! *(Caliban drinks.)* You, drink more. *(Caliban refuses.)* You no more thirsty? *(Stephano drinks.)* Me always thirsty! *(Stephano and Trinculo drink.)*

STEPHANO: Trinculo, you know I used to be prejudiced against shipwrecks, but I was wrong. They're not bad at all.

TRINCULO: That's true. It seems to make things taste better afterwards...

STEPHANO: Not to mention the fact that it's got rid of a lot of old farts that were always keeping the world down! May they rest in peace! But then, you liked them, didn't you, all those kings and dukes, all those noblemen! Oh, I served them well enough, you've got to earn your drink somehow... But I could never stand them, ever — understand? Never. Trinculo, my friend, I'm a long-time believer in the republic...you might as well say it: I'm a died-in-the-wool believer in the people first, a republican in my guts! Down with tyrants!

TRINCULO: Which reminds me...If, as it would seem, the King and the Duke are dead, there's a crown and a throne up for grabs around here...

STEPHANO: By God, you're right! Smart thinking, Trinculo! So, I appoint myself heir...I crown myself king of the island.

TRINCULO: *(sarcastically)* Sure you do! And why you, may I ask? I'm the one who thought of it first, that crown!

STEPHANO: Look, Trinculo, don't be silly! I mean, really: just take a look at yourself! What's the first thing a king needs? Bearing. Presence. And if I've got anything, it's that. Which isn't true for everyone. So, I am the King!

CALIBAN: Long live the King!

STEPHANO: It's a miracle...he can talk! And what's more, he talks sense! O brave savage! *(He embraces Caliban.)* You see, my dear Trinculo, the people has spoken! Vox populi, vox Dei... But please, don't be upset. Stephano is magnanimous and will never abandon his friend Trinculo, the friend who stood by him in his trials. Trinculo, we've eaten rough bread together, we've drunk rot-gut wine together. I want to do something for you. I shall appoint you Marshal. But we're forgetting our brave savage... It's a scientific miracle! He can talk!

CALIBAN: Yes, Sire. My enthusiasm has restored my speech. Long live the King! But beware the usurper!

STEPHANO: Usurper? Who? Trinculo?

CALIBAN: No, the other one... Prospero!

STEPHANO: Prospero? Don't know him.

CALIBAN: Well, you see, this island used to belong to me, except that a man named Prospero cheated me of it. I'm perfectly willing to give you my right to it, but the only thing is, you'll have to fight Prospero for it.

STEPHANO: That is of no matter, brave savage. It's a bargain! I'll get rid of this Prospero for you in two shakes.

CALIBAN: Watch out, he's powerful.

STEPHANO: ˙My dear savage, I eat a dozen Prosperos like that for breakfast every day. But say no more, say no more! Trinculo, take command of the troops! Let us march upon the foe!

TRINCULO: Yes, forward march! But first, a drink. We will need all our strength and vigor.

CALIBAN: Let's drink, my new-found friends, and let us sing. Let us sing of winning the day and of an end to tyranny.
    (Singing)

Black pecking creature of the savannas
The quetzal measures out the new day
solid and lively
in its haughty armor.
Zing! the determined hummingbird
revels in the flower's depths,
going crazy, getting drunk,
a lyrebird gathers up our ravings,
Freedom hi-day! Freedom hi-day!

STEPHANO and TRINCULO: *(Together)* Freedom hi-day! Freedom hi-day!

CALIBAN:

The ringdove dallies amid the trees,
wandering the islands, here it rests —
The white blossoms of the miconia
Mingle with the violet blood of ripe berries
And blood stains your plumage,
traveller!
Lying here after a weary day
We listen to it:
Freedom hi-day! Freedom hi-day!

STEPHANO: Okay, monster...enough crooning. Singing makes a man thirsty. Let's drink instead. Here, have some more...spirits create higher spirits... *(Filling a glass.)* Lead the way, O bountiful wine! Soldiers, forward march! Or rather...no: At ease! Night is falling, the fireflies twinkle, the crickets chirp, all nature makes its brek-ke-ke-kek! And since night has fallen, let us take advantage of it to gather our forces and regain our strength, which has been sorely tried by the unusually...copious emotions of the day. And tomorrow, at dawn, with a new spring in our step, we'll have the tyrant's hide. Good night, gentlemen. *(He falls asleep and begins to snore.)*

SCENE 3

Prospero's cave

PROSPERO: So then, Ariel! Where are the gods and goddesses? They'd better get a move on! And all of them! I want all of them to take part in the entertainment I have planned for our dear children. Why do I say "entertainment"? Because starting today I want to inculcate in them the spectacle of tomorrow's world: logic, beauty, harmony, the foundations for which I have laid down by my own will-power. Unfortunately, alas, at my age it's time to stop thinking of deeds and to begin thinking of passing on... Enter, then!

Gods and Goddesses enter.

JUNO: Honor and riches to you! Long continuance and increasing long life and honored issue! Juno sings to you her blessings!

CERES: May scarcity and want shun you! That is Ceres' blessing on you.

IRIS: *(beckoning to the Nymphs)* Nymphs, come help to celebrate here a contact of true love.

Nymphs enter and dance.

PROSPERO: My thanks, Goddesses, and my thanks to you, Iris. Thank you for your good wishes.

Gods and Goddesses continue their dance.

FERDINAND: What a splendid and majestic vision! May I be so bold to think these spirits?

PROSPERO: Yes, spirits which by my art I have from their confines called to greet you and to bless you.

Enter Eshu.

MIRANDA: But who is that? He doesn't look very benevolent! If I weren't afraid of blaspheming, I'd say he was a devil rather than a god.

ESHU: *(Laughing)* You are not mistaken, fair lady. God to my friends, the Devil to my enemies! And lots of laughs for all!

PROSPERO: *(Softly)* Ariel must have made a mistake. Is my magic getting rusty? *(Aloud)* What are you doing here? Who invited you? I don't like such loose behavior, even from a god!

ESHU: But that's just the point...no one invited me... And that wasn't very nice! Nobody remembered poor Eshu! So poor Eshu came anyway. Hihihi! So how about something to drink? *(Without waiting for a reply, he pours a drink.)* ...Your liquor's not bad. However, I must say I prefer dogs! *(Looking at Iris)* I see that shocks the little lady, but to each his own. Some prefer chickens, others prefer goats. I'm not too fond of chickens, myself. But if you're talking about a black dog...think of poor Eshu!

PROSPERO: Get out! Go away! We will have none of your grimaces and buffoonery in this noble assembly. (*He makes a magic sign.*)

ESHU: I'm going, boss, I'm going... But not without a little song in honor of the bride and the noble company, as you say.

>
> Eshu can play many tricks,
> Give him twenty dogs!
> You will see his dirty tricks.
>
> Eshu plays a trick on the Queen
> And makes her so upset that she runs
> Naked into the street
>
> Eshu plays a trick on a bride,
> And on the day of the wedding
> She gets into the wrong bed!
>
> Eshu can throw a stone yesterday
> And kill a bird today.
> He can make a mess out of order and vice-versa.
> Ah, Eshu is a wonderful bad joke.
> Eshu is not the man to carry a heavy load.
> His head comes to a point. When he dances
> He doesn't move his shoulders...
> Oh, Eshu is a merry elf!
>
> Eshu is a merry elf,
> And he can whip you with his dick,
> He can whip you,
> He can whip you...

CERES: My dear Iris, don't you find that song quite obscene?

JUNO: It's disgusting! It's quite intolerable...if he keeps on, I'm leaving!

IRIS: It's like Liber, or Priapus!

JUNO: Don't mention that name in my presence!

ESHU: *(continuing to sing)*

> ...*with his dick*
> *He can whip you, whip you...*

JUNO: Oh! Can't someone get rid of him? I'm not staying here!

ESHU: Okay, okay...Eshu will go. Farewell, my dear colleagues!

Gods and Goddesses exit.

PROSPERO: He's gone...what a relief! But alas, the harm is done! I am perturbed... My old brain is confused. Power! Power! Alas! All this will one day fade, like foam, like a cloud, like all the world. And what is power, if I cannot calm my own fears? But come! My power has gone cold. *(Calling)* Ariel!

ARIEL: *(runs in)* What is it, Sire?

PROSPERO: Caliban is alive, he is plotting, he is getting a guerrilla force together and you—you don't say a word! Well, take care of him. Snakes, scorpions, porcupines, all stinging poisonous creatures, he is to be spared nothing! His punishment must be exemplary. Oh, and don't forget the mud and mosquitoes!

ARIEL: Master, let me intercede for him and beg your indulgence. You've got to understand: he's a rebel.

PROSPERO: By his insubordination he's calling into question the whole order of the world. Maybe the Divinity can afford to let him get away with it, but I have a sense of responsibility!

ARIEL: Very well, Master.

PROSPERO: But a thought: arrange some glass trinkets, some trumpery and some second-hand clothes too...but colorful ones...by the side of the road along which General Caliban and his troops are travelling. Savages adore loud, gaudy clothes...

ARIEL: Master...

PROSPERO: You're going to make me angry. There's nothing to understand. There is a punishment to be meted out. I will not compromise with evil. Hurry! Unless you want to be the next to feel my wrath.

SCENE 4

*In the wild; night is drawing to a close; the murmurings of
the spirits of the tropical forest are heard.*

VOICE I: Fly!

VOICE: Here!

VOICE I: Ant!

VOICE II: Here.

VOICE I: Vulture!

VOICE II: Here.

VOICE I: Soft-shelled crab, calao, crab, hummingbird!

VOICES: Here. Here. Here.

VOICE I: Cramp, crime, fang, opossum!

VOICE II: Kra. Kra. Kra.

VOICE I: Huge hedgehog, you will be our sun today.
Shaggy, taloned, stubborn. May it burn! Moon, my fat
spider, my big dreamcat, go to sleep, my velvet one.

VOICES: *(singing)*

> *King-ay*
> *King-ay*

Von-von
Maloto
Vloom-vloom!

The sun rises. Ariel's band vanishes. Caliban stands for a moment, rubbing his eyes.

CALIBAN: *(rises and searches the bushes)* Have to think about getting going again. Away, snakes, scorpions, porcupines! All stinging, biting, sticking beasts! Sting, fever, venom, away! Or if you really want to lick me, do it with a gentle tongue, like the toad whose pure drool soothes me with sweet dreams of the future. For it is for you, for all of us, that I go forth today to face the common enemy. Yes, hereditary and common. Look, a hedgehog! Sweet little thing... How can any animal—any natural animal, if I may put it that way—go against me on the day I'm setting forth to conquer Prospero! Unimaginable! Prospero is the Anti-Nature! And I say, down with Anti-Nature! And does the porcupine bristle his spines at that? No, he smoothes them down! That's nature! It's kind and gentle, in a word. You've just got to know how to deal with it. So come on, the way is clear! Off we go!

The band sets out. Caliban marches forward singing his battle song:

> *Shango carries a big stick,*
> *He strikes and money expires!*
> *He strikes and lies expire!*
> *He strikes and larceny expires!*
> *Shango, Shango ho!*

Shango is the gatherer of the rain,
He passes, wrapped in his fiery cloak,
His horse's hoofs strike lighting
On the pavements of the sky!
Shango is a great knight!
Shango, Shango ho!

The roar of the sea can be heard.

STEPHANO: Tell me, brave savage, what is that noise? It sounds like the roaring of a beast at bay.

CALIBAN: Not at bay...more like on the prowl... Don't worry, it's a pal of mine.

STEPHANO: You are very closemouthed about the company you keep.

CALIBAN: And yet it helps me breathe. That's why I call it a pal. Sometimes it sneezes, and a drop falls on my forehead and cools me with its salt, or blesses me...

STEPHANO: I don't understand. You aren't drunk, are you?

CALIBAN: Come on! It's that howling impatient thing that suddenly appears in a clap of thunder like some God and hits you in the face, that rises up out of the very depths of the abyss and smites you with its fury! It's the sea!

STEPHANO: Odd country! And an odd baptism!

CALIBAN: But the best is still the wind and the songs it sings...its dirty sigh when it rustles through the bushes, or its triumphant chant when it passes by breaking trees, remnants of their terror in its beard.

STEPHANO: The savage is delirious, he's raving mad! Tough luck, Trinculo, our savage is playing without a full deck!

TRINCULO: I'm kind of shuffling myself... In other words, I'm exhausted. I never knew such hard going! Savage, even your mud is muddier.

CALIBAN: That isn't mud...it's something Prospero's dreamed up.

TRINCULO: There's a savage for you...everything's always caused by someone. The sun is Prospero's smile. The rain is the tear in Prospero's eye... And I suppose the mud is Prospero's shit. And what about the mosquitoes? What are they, may I ask? Zzzzz, Zzzzz...do you hear them? My face is being eaten off!

CALIBAN: Those aren't mosquitoes. It's some kind of gas that stings your nose and throat and makes you itch. It's another of Prospero's tricks. It's part of his arsenal.

STEPHANO: What do you mean by that?

CALIBAN: I mean his anti-riot arsenal! He's got a lot of gadgets like these...gadgets to make you deaf, to blind you, to make you sneeze, to make you cry...

TRINCULO: And to make you slip! Shit! This is some fix you've got us in! I can't take anymore...I'm going to sit down!

STEPHANO: Come on, Trinculo, show a little courage! We're engaged in a mobile ground manoeuvre here, and you know what that means: drive, initiatives, split-second decisions to meet new eventualities, and — above all — mobility. Let's go! Up you get! Mobility!

TRINCULO: But my feet are bleeding!

STEPHANO: Get up or I'll knock you down! *(Trinculo begins to walk again.)* But tell me, my good savage, this usurper of yours seems very well protected. It might be dangerous to attack him!

CALIBAN: You mustn't underestimate him. You mustn't overestimate him, either...he's showing his power, but he's doing it mostly to impress us.

STEPHANO: No matter. Trinculo, we must take precautions. Axiom: never underestimate the enemy. Here, pass me that bottle. I can always use it as a club.

Highly colored clothing is seen, hanging from a rope.

TRINCULO: Right, Stephano. On with the battle. Victory means loot. And there's a foretaste of it...look at that fine wardrobe! Trinculo, my friend, methinks you are going to put on those britches...they'll replace your torn trousers.

STEPHANO: Look out, Trinculo...one move and I'll knock you down. As your lord and master I have the first pick, and with those britches I'm exercising my feudal rights...

TRINCULO: I saw them first!

STEPHANO: The King gets first pick in every country in the world.

TRINCULO: That's tyranny, Stephano. I'm not going to let you get away with it.

They fight.

CALIBAN: Let it alone, fool. I tell you about winning your dignity, and you start fighting over hand-me-downs! *(To himself)* To think I'm stuck with these jokers! What an idiot I am! How could I ever have thought I could create the Revolution with swollen guts and fat faces! Oh well! History won't blame me for not having been able to win my freedom all by myself. It's you and me, Prospero! *(Weapon in hand, he advances on Prospero who has just appeared.)*

PROSPERO: *(bares his chest to him)* Strike! Go on, strike! Strike your Master, your benefactor! Don't tell me you're going to spare him!

Caliban raises his arm, but hesitates.

Go on! You don't dare! See, you're nothing but an animal...you don't know how to kill.

CALIBAN: Defend yourself! I'm not a murderer.

PROSPERO: *(very calm)* The worse for you. You've lost your chance. Stupid as a slave! And now, enough of this farce. *(Calling)* Ariel! *(to Ariel)* Ariel, take charge of the prisoners!

Caliban, Trinculo and Stephano are taken prisoners.

SCENE 5

> *Prospero's cave. Miranda and Ferdinand are playing chess.*

MIRANDA: Sir, I think you're cheating.

FERDINAND: And what if I told you that I would not do so for twenty kingdoms?

MIRANDA: I would not believe a word of it, but I would forgive you. Now, be honest...you did cheat!

FERDINAND: I'm pleased that you were able to tell. *(Laughing)* That makes me less worried at the thought that soon you will be leaving your innocent flowery kingdom for my less-innocent world of men.

MIRANDA: Oh, you know that, hitched to your star, I would brave the demons of hell!

> *The Nobles enter.*

ALONSO: My son! This marriage! The thrill of it has struck me dumb! The thrill and the joy!

GONZALO: A happy ending to a most opportune shipwreck!

ALONSO: A unique one, indeed, for it can legitimately be described as such.

GONZALO: Look at them! Isn't it wonderful! I've been too

choked up to speak, or I would have already told these children all the joy my old heart feels at seeing them living love's young dream and cherishing each other so tenderly.

ALONSO: *(to Ferdinand and Miranda)* My children, give me your hands. May the Lord bless you.

GONZALO: Amen! Amen!

Enter Prospero.

PROSPERO: Thank you, Gentlemen, for having agreed to join in this little family party. Your presence has brought us comfort and joy. However, you must now think of getting some rest. Tomorrow morning, you will recover your vessels — they are undamaged — and your men, who I can guarantee are safe, hale and hearty. I shall return with you to Europe, and I can promise you — I should say: promise us — a rapid sail and propitious winds.

GONZALO: God be praised! We are delighted...delighted and overcome! What a happy, what a memorable day! With one voyage Antonio has found a brother, his brother has found a dukedom, his daughter has found a husband. Alonso has regained his son and gained a daughter. And what else?... Anyway, I am the only one whose emotion prevents him from knowing what he's saying...

PROSPERO: The proof of that, my fine Gonzalo, is that you are forgetting someone: Ariel, my loyal servant. *(Turning to Ariel)* Yes, Ariel, today you will be free. Go, my sweet. I hope you will not be bored.

ARIEL: Bored! I fear that the days will seem all too short!
There, where the Cecropia gloves its impatient hands with silver,
Where the ferns free the stubborn black stumps
from their scored bodies with a green cry —
There where the intoxicating berry ripens the visit
 of the wild ring-dove
through the throat of that musical bird
I shall let fall
one by one,
each more pleasing than the last
four notes so sweet that the last
will give rise to a yearning
in the heart of the most forgetful slaves
yearning for freedom!

PROSPERO: Come, come. All the same, you are not going
to set my world on fire with your music, I trust!

ARIEL: *(with intoxication)*
Or on some stony plane
perched on an agave stalk
I shall be the thrush that launches
its mocking cry
to the benighted field-hand
"Dig, nigger! Dig, nigger!"
and the lightened agave will
straighten from my flight,
a solemn flag.

PROSPERO: That is a very unsettling agenda! Go! Scram!
Before I change my mind!

Enter Stephano, Trinculo, Caliban.

GONZALO: Sire, here are your people.

PROSPERO: Oh no, not all of them! Some are yours.

ALONSO: True. There's that fool Trinculo and that unspeakable Stephano.

STEPHANO: The very ones, Sire, in person. We throw ourselves at your merciful feet.

ALONSO: What became of you?

STEPHANO: Sire, we were walking in the forest — no, it was in the fields — when we saw some perfectly respectable clothing blowing in the wind. We thought it only right to collect them and we were returning them to their rightful owner when a frightful adventure befell us...

TRINCULO: Yes, we were mistaken for thieves and treated accordingly.

STEPHANO: Yes, Sire, it is the most dreadful thing that could happen to an honest man: victims of a judicial error, a miscarriage of justice!

PROSPERO: Enough! Today is a day to be benevolent, and it will do no good to try to talk sense to you in the state you're in... Leave us. Go sleep it off, drunkards. We raise sail tomorrow.

TRINCULO: Raise sail! But that's what we do all the time, Sire, Stephano and I...at least, we raise our glasses, from dawn till dusk till dawn.. The hard part is putting them down, landing, as you might say.

PROSPERO: Scoundrels! If only life could bring you to the safe harbors of Temperance and Sobriety!

ALONSO: *(indicating Caliban)* That is the strangest creature I've ever seen!

PROSPERO: And the most devilish too!

GONZALO: What's that? Devilish! You've reprimanded him, preached at him, you've ordered and made him obey and you say he is still indomitable!

PROSPERO: Honest Gonzalo, it is as I have said.

GONZALO: Well — and forgive me, Counsellor, if I give counsel — on the basis of my long experience the only thing left is exorcism. "Begone, unclean spirit, in the name of the Father, of the Son and of the Holy Ghost." That's all there is to it!

Caliban bursts out laughing.

GONZALO: You were absolutely right! And more so that you thought... He's not just a rebel, he's a real tough customer! *(To Caliban)* So much the worse for you, my friend. I have tried to save you. I give up. I leave you to the secular arm!

PROSPERO: Come here, Caliban. Have you got anything to say in your own defence? Take advantage of my good humor. I'm in a forgiving mood today.

CALIBAN: I'm not interested in defending myself. My only regret is that I've failed.

PROSPERO: What were you hoping for?

CALIBAN: To get back my island and regain my freedom.

PROSPERO: And what would you do all alone here on this island, haunted by the devil, tempest tossed?

CALIBAN: First of all, I'd get rid of you! I'd spit you out, all your works and pomps! Your "white" magic!

PROSPERO: That's a fairly negative program...

CALIBAN: You don't understand it...I say I'm going to spit you out, and that's very positive...

PROSPERO: Well, the world is really upside down... We've seen everything now: Caliban as a dialectician! However, in spite of everything I'm fond of you, Caliban. Come, let's make peace. We've lived together for ten years and worked side by side! Ten years count for something, after all! We've ended up by becoming compatriots!

CALIBAN: You know very well that I'm not interested in peace. I'm interested in being free! Free, you hear?

PROSPERO: It's odd...no matter what you do, you won't succeed in making me believe that I'm a tyrant!

CALIBAN: Understand what I say, Prospero:
For years I bowed my head
for years I took it, all of it—
your insults, your ingratitude...
and worst of all, more degrading than all the rest,
your condescension.
But now, it's over!
Over, do you hear?
Of course, at the moment
You're still stronger than I am.
But I don't give a damn for your power
or for your dogs or your police or your inventions!
And do you know why?
It's because I know I'll get you.
I'll impale you! And on a stake that you've sharpened
yourself!
You'll have impaled yourself!
Prospero, you're a great magician:
you're an old hand at deception.
And you lied to me so much,
about the world, about myself,
that you ended up by imposing on me
an image of myself:
underdeveloped, in your words, undercompetent
that's how you made me see myself!
And I hate that image...and it's false!
But now I know you, you old cancer,
And I also know myself!

And I know that one day
my bare fist, just that,
will be enough to crush your world!
The old world is crumbling down!

Isn't it true? Just look!
It even bores you to death.
And by the way...you have a chance to get it over with:
You can pick up and leave.
You can go back to Europe.
But the hell you will!
I'm sure you won't leave.
You make me laugh with your "mission"!
Your "vocation"!
Your vocation is to hassle me.
And that's why you'll stay,
just like those guys who founded the colonies
and who now can't live anywhere else.
You're just an old addict, that's what you are!

PROSPERO: Poor Caliban! You know that you're headed towards your own ruin. You're sliding towards suicide! You know I will be the stronger, and stronger all the time. I pity you!

CALIBAN: And I hate you!

PROSPERO: Beware! My generosity has its limits.

CALIBAN: *(shouting)*

> *Shango marches with strength*
> *along his path, the sky!*

Shango is a fire-bearer,
his steps shake the heavens
and the earth
Shango, Shango, ho!

PROSPERO: I have uprooted the oak and raised the sea,
I have caused the mountain to tremble and have bared my
chest to adversity.
With Jove I have traded thunderbolt for thunderbolt.
Better yet — from a brutish monster I have made man!
But ah! To have failed to find the path to man's heart...
if that be where man is.
(to Caliban)
Well, I hate you as well!
For it is you who have made me
doubt myself for the first time.
(to the Nobles)
...My friends, come near. We must say farewell... I shall not
be going with you. My fate is here: I shall not run from it.

ANTONIO: What, Sire?

PROSPERO: Hear me well.
I am not in any ordinary sense a master,
as this savage thinks,
but rather the conductor of a boundless score:
this isle,
summoning voices, I alone,
and mingling them at my pleasure,
arranging out of confusion
one intelligible line.
Without me, who would be able to draw music from all that?
This isle is mute without me.

My duty, thus, is here,
and here I shall stay.

GONZALO: Oh day full rich in miracles!

PROSPERO: Do not be distressed. Antonio, be you the
lieutenant of my goods and make use of them as procurator
until that time when Ferdinand and Miranda may take
effective possession of them, joining them with the
Kingdom of Naples. Nothing of that which has been set for
them must be postponed: Let their marriage be celebrated
at Naples with all royal splendor. Honest Gonzalo, I place
my trust in your word. You shall stand as father to our
princess at this ceremony.

GONZALO: Count on me, Sire.

PROSPERO: Gentlemen, farewell.

They exit.

And now, Caliban, it's you and me!
What I have to tell you will be brief:
Ten times, a hundred times, I've tried to save you,
above all from yourself.
But you have always answered me with wrath
and venom,
like the opossum that pulls itself up by its own tail
the better to bite the hand that tears it from the darkness.
Well, my boy, I shall set aside my indulgent nature
and henceforth I will answer your violence
with violence!

Time passes, symbolized by the curtain's being lowered halfway and reraised. In semi-darkness Prospero appears, aged and weary. His gestures are jerky and automatic, his speech weak, toneless, trite.

PROSPERO: Odd, but for some time now we seem to be overrun with opossums. They're everywhere. Peccarys, wild boar, all this unclean nature! But mainly opossums. Those eyes! The vile grins they have! It's as though the jungle was laying siege to the cave... But I shall stand firm...I shall not let my work perish! *(Shouting)* I shall protect civilization! *(He fires in all directions.)* They're done for! Now, this way I'll be able to have some peace and quiet for a while. But it's cold. Odd how the climate's changed. Cold on this island... Have to think about making a fire... Well, Caliban, old fellow, it's just us two now, here on the island...only you and me. You and me. You-me...me-you! What in the hell is he up to? *(Shouting)* Caliban!

In the distance, above the sound of the surf and the chirping of birds, we hear snatches of Caliban's song:

FREEDOM HI-DAY, FREEDOM HI-DAY!

∾

ANNEX

Literal Translations of Songs

Ariel's Song (Act I, scene 2)

Chestnut horses of the sand
They bite out the place
Where the waves expire in
Pure languor.
Where the waves die
Here come all,
Join hands
And dance.

Blond sands,
What fire!
Languorous waves,
Pure expiration.
Here lips lick and lick again
Our wounds.

The waves make a waterline...
Nothing is, all is becoming...
The season is close and strange

The eye is a fine pearl
The heart of coral, the bone of coral,
There, at the waterline
As the sea swells within us.

Trinculo's Song (Act III, Scene 2)

Virginia, with tears in my eyes
I bid you farewell.
We're off to Mexico,
Straight into the setting sun.

With sails unfurled, my dear love,
It torments me to leave you,
A tempest is brewing
Some storm is howling
That will carry off the entire crew!

Stephano's Song (Act III, Scene 2)

(Obviously an old sea chanty or Césaire's adaptation of one)

Bravely on, guys, step it lively,
bravely on, farewell Bordeaux,
To Cape Horn, it won't be hot,
Off to hunt the whale.

More than one of us will lose his skin
Farewell misery, farewell ship.
The ones who return with all flags flying
Will be the first-rate sailors...